This Notebook Belongs To:

_____

_____

SO APPARENTLY

• • • • • • • • •

I HAVE AN

"ATTITUDE"

Time to head back to Amazon to order another book. If you enjoyed this journal, we hope you will share your opinion by leaving a review on Amazon.
Thank you,
Cleo Press

CPSIA information can be obtained
at www.ICGtesting.com
Printed in the USA
LVHW081039141119
636964LV00014B/4575/P